From Zero to 3 Properties In 3 Years

A Rentvestors Guide to Building a $2,000 per month Cash flow Positive Portfolio.

by

Louis Strange

& Jayden Vecchio

http://www.therentvestingpodcast.com.au/

This book is licensed for your personal use only and should not be taken as advice. Please consider the information contained within as general in nature as it does not consider your individual situation. This book may not be re-sold or given away to other people. If you'd like to share this book with another person, please purchase an additional copy for each person you share it with.

Copyright © 2017 The Rentvesting Podcast. All rights reserved. Including the right to reproduce this book or portions thereof, in any form. No part of this text may be reproduced in any form without the express written permission of the author.

Version 2017.4.26

Contents

- Our Mission 4
- About the Strategy 5
- Step 1: Get your deposit 6
- Step 2: Finding your first property 11
- Step 3: Work towards your next property 15
- Step 4: Buy property 2 18
- Step 5: Building deposit number 3 20
- Step 6: Buy property 3 22
- Step 7: You're earning $2,000 per month 23
- What are the risks involved? 25
- Time to get started…. 27

Our Mission

Our vision is to help property owners (or aspiring ones) cut through the hype, look at the facts and educate themselves to make smarter property decisions. We want to help you avoid making the same mistakes we have over the years, and grow your wealth - but it all starts with you.

It is not hard to achieve anything that you start, as in most cases it is YOU who stands in your own way! Being in debt, not taking time to travel or spend with your family are things that are solely in your control at the end of the day. Sure, the banks may be on your back or you had a bad day at the office, but this is something that you can change! So stop getting in the way of your dreams and start doing! This is easier said than done but don't give up hope!

We have put together this guide for you to improve your knowledge of property using simple and effective techniques we have described, and ultimately help you – Live Where you Want, and Invest Where You can Afford.

- Louis Strange & Jayden Vecchio.

About the Strategy

This is an accelerated strategy on the road to 3 investment properties within 3 years. We know you are busy so we won't waste your time with any pie in the sky dreams, but lay out the strategy that so many people follow along with tips on how to save you time and some financial headaches in the long term.

This strategy works by buying an investment property, then using that property to help accelerate your next purchase so that you can get your 3 properties in 3 years. There is a proven system to guide you from start to finish in everything you do! The good news is that almost ANYONE can do this; you just have to be disciplined! Too many people just hope and wish that they will get what they want along the way. But there is a simple formula!

This strategy uses leverage in both time and money to get the most out of your ability to accumulate wealth. Leverage your time through professionals to do the leg work for you and reduce your stress. Leverage your money to help maximise returns and deductions.

This strategy uses discipline. To get to your goal of 3 in 3, you will need to be disciplined. Discipline through making your savings work for you and disciplined in removing your emotions and spontaneous purchases which aren't in the budget.

Now that you have the basics, let's move onto the steps to start your property journey!

Step 1: Get your deposit

This will be the hardest step for most people as property prices increase and lending requirements tighten, however it can be achieved for those who really want to make it happen.

A general rule of thumb is to aim for around 20% of the property value as a deposit. Due to this, it is better for most people to start out with an investment property with a lower value than what you would look at for purchasing as a home to live in. Don't get bogged down with this. If you live in an area where property is overvalued, then getting a 20% deposit on a $1,000,000 property will be hard to reach for 99% of us in a 12-month timeframe. So aim for a property that is undervalued, in an undervalued area.

There are a few options available to generate the level of deposit you will need. Options to get deposit vary from situation to situation:

Home equity – If you have equity in property that you already own (either your home or an existing investment property) then you may not need to save anything further. You have the ability to access any extra equity in a property, all the way up to 80% of the current valuation.

This process involves a refinance or your personal place of residence, or investment property to create an additional investment loan. If this option is available then happy days, you can most likely shorten the time period to purchase your first property.

Savings – Okay, this one will be less pleasant than the first option requiring some tightening of the belt, so to speak. To acquire a home deposit in a period of 12 months is a great feat, but it is possible. One of the best strategies is to implement the 50/25/25 Budget Rule! This is where 50% of your income is spent on essential living expenses, 25% is sent on lifestyle spending and the remaining 25% is spent on savings. It will take some time to get used to but once it is a habit, it is your key to this strategy, and any future wealth building strategy.

You need to plan to invest for your future. This will take some time, but it is worth it. Why give someone else your hard earned dollars, give it to yourself first.

Let's take a case study to explain this a little better. The following are different amounts you will need to save in a 12 month period to achieve different levels of deposit. Assuming you have nothing, it will take you a year at the following amounts to save for a deposit (assuming the funds are kept in cash earning around 2% interest).

Property Price	Deposit required (20%)	Monthly savings
$200,000	$40,000	$3,303
$300,000	$60,000	$4,955
$400,000	$80,000	$6,607

I know these numbers seem high but don't give up there. Your ability to save is not your capability to save. Everyone is capable of saving, but depending on your experience with money your ability may be hampered due to habitual behaviours. This is where you need to shift gears and get into savings mode. There will be a few 'sacrifices' on those otherwise discretionary spending but what is more important to you, a coffee or your dream of getting an investment property? It seems unreasonable to some people but this has become a society expectation of no longer saving. Have a look at the historical household saving rates:

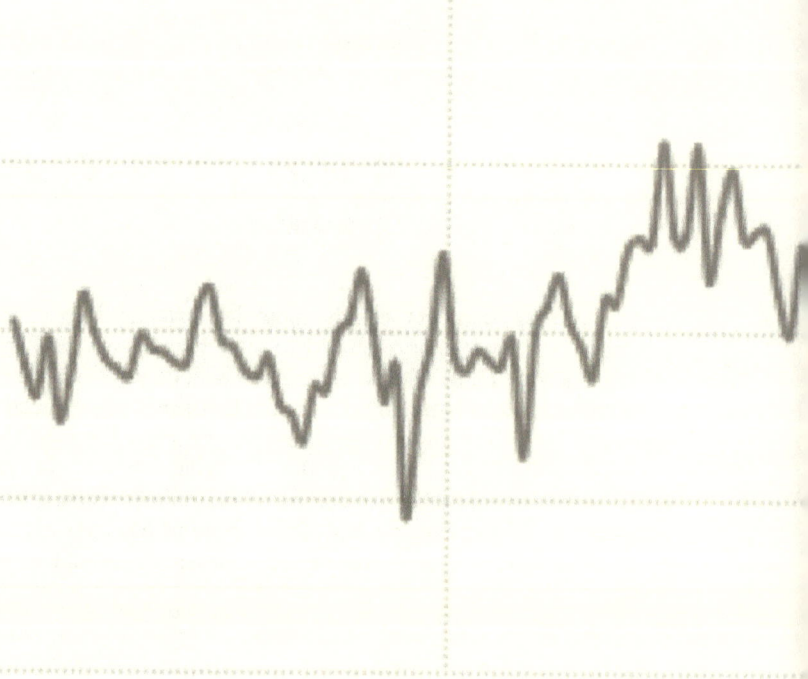

AUSTRALIA HOUSEHOLD SAVING RAT

1969

Pre GFC household saving rates were at their lowest in the past 40 years. This was the prime example of a spend-spend culture where the average rate was 0% in the early 2000s. This was a massive decline from 30 years ago, where the average household savings rates were almost 20%.

This rate has risen since the shock of the GFC as households have become more conservative (due to previous losses), up to approximately 10%. but this is the average. Don't you want to be above average?

Let's have a look at a working example. Take a couple where one earns $100,000 and the other $60,000. They have around $20,000 currently saved and want to buy their first investment in a 12-month period. Their incomes look like this

	Person 1	Person 2
Salary	$ 100,000.00	$ 60,000.00
Assessable income	$ 100,000.00	$ 60,000.00
Tax payable	$ 24,946.63	$ 11,046.68
Medicare levy	$ 2,000.00	$ 1,200.00
Total tax	$ 26,946.63	$ 12,246.68
Income after tax	$ 73,053.37	$ 47,753.32
Combined AT Income	$ 120,807.69	

For this couple, if they follow the 50/25/25 rule their income will be split as follows:

Living expenses	$	60,403.35
Discretionary spending	$	30,201.67
Savings	$	30,201.67

This couple have the ability to save at least $2,517 per month. For even faster savings, why not cut down on the dinners, coffees and other items which may seem small, but when regular, add up to thousands per year without you noticing! I know that some households may not be on these levels of income, and that is okay. It doesn't mean that you can't still implement a strategy that works for you. You can either purchase a lower valued property, requiring a lower deposit, or extend the saving period out to 18 months.

Tracking your goal!

I know I am not alone when I say that my goals for 2016 were my goals for 2015, where I didn't manage some of my goals from 2014. The best way to manage to achieve any goal is so simple it hurts me to think about the number of times I failed to reach an annual goal. So, if your goal is for the year, why not break it down to 52 saving targets. I hope we can all agree that there are 52 weeks in the year. This is the number I use when looking at savings. If you need to save $40,000 for a deposit, break it down into small chunks. This allows you to use 52 lots of saving $769 which can be easily tracked and managed.

Use our excel sheet to track your goal each week. Get your target in place and track and adjust along the way.

Another great way to get to this goal is using the technology to automate your savings. Set up monthly direct debits from your pay into a separate savings account. This will allow for the out of sight, out of mind mentality to enable you to generate your savings.

Step 2: Finding your first property

Now that you have your deposit in place, it is time to look for your first property. This can be a daunting step for most people and the more daunting it feels, the less likely you will take the plunge, especially if this is your first home purchase. Following a simple strategy can help remove some of the anxiety, time and stress of the process.

Outsource to a professional!

Professional #1: Buyers' agent

With the rise in the demand for property has come a new type of professional called Buyers' Agents. They are licensed professionals that specialise in searching, evaluating and negotiating the purchase of a property on your behalf. Think of them as a real estate agent that help you buy a property instead of sell.

Rather than trying to do all the research yourself around what is the best area for growth, low vacancy rates or best rental yields, buyers' agents have all of this information on hand as it is what they do day-to-day.

This can also help remove the emotion from this purchase, as remember an investment should have no emotional or sentimental value to you. It is not for you to live in but for you to get onto? the property market at an attractive price and with good potential for rental returns.

How much deposit you have managed to save will be the ultimate decision on what price you should be looking at when making the purchase.

Typical process:

- Strategy – The first step is to explain what your criteria is around the purchase so they can help formulate the overall plan. You need a clear picture of what you are after such as budget, rental incomes, vacancy rates along with your timeline of owning the property. Property should be viewed as a long-term investment as anything can happen in the short term but property should increase in value over the longer term, typically 5 to 7 years.

- Research – Next the agent should help educate you on the key suburbs you should target based on your criteria. They typically have access to a large database which the average individual has trouble to access.

- Shortlist – Based around your criteria the agent will summarise a few properties which will be the best fit for your situation. They typically have an extensive network of sales agents to help find suitable properties.

- Agree on a property – Once you have found the ideal property, the agent will do a valuation on the property to give a clear indication of the current market value. This helps to gain a true understanding around what the property is really worth, not what it is being sold for. This level of knowledge will avoid the pitfall of paying too much for a property.

- Negotiate and secure – The last step is where the buyers' agent can really add value. By having them do the negotiation they can help get the property for the price you want, helping you avoid spending more than you want by making an emotional purchase. They also help coordinate the required pest and building inspections and facilitate the exchange of contracts.

There will be costs involved in this, typically in the form of commission based on a percentage of the purchase price. While nobody likes to pay for things, the time this can save you along with avoiding purchasing a property in an area which is unlikely to give you what you want it can be better to pay to avoid this. As the saying goes, you get what you pay for.

Professional #2: Mortgage broker

Now that you have your property in mind and your deposit ready to go, you need the finance. This is where a mortgage broker can come in handy. A mortgage broker works as an intermediary between yourself and the banks when it comes to borrowing a mortgage.

The typical process is that they gather your data such as incomes, assets and supporting documentation and provide these to a number of lenders to see who can get you the best rate and structure for the finance. The major benefit of a mortgage broker is that they are working for you, not the banks. Basically, they do all the legwork for you and provide a quick and easy comparison between your lending options. They can also help provide some advice around how to best structure a loan and make repayments to reduce the life of the loan.

The best structure for your loan to make this strategy work looks something like the following:

- Level of debt – 80% to avoid lenders mortgage insurances in most cases. If you can get away with it, you can try for 10%.
- Repayments – Interest only payments are better, not only from a cashflow point of view to help you continue saving but also from a deductibility point of view. Any principle repayments are not deductible.
- Offset account – having a genuine offset account against your property will help save interest repayments while still allowing access to the funds to purchase property two.
- Variable rate – allows flexibility of additional repayment as opposed to a fixed rate which does not.

The best part about using a broker is that it costs you nothing and saves you a lot of time and effort.

Professional #3: Property manager

Once the property is purchased, think about hiring a property manager. These are professionals who tend to the property for a fee. Their typical duties are those of a normal landlord while coordinating with your wishes. They help collect rents, pay necessary expenses, inspect the property on a regular basis and arrange for any maintenance or repairs to take place. They also help to find tenants for you so you don't have to worry about getting the property filled every few months.

If you are interstate or just time poor like most of us, it is worth it to have someone deal with the day to day running of the property.

Let's have a look at an example of this. Our couple from before have managed to save their deposit of $50,000 and therefore can purchase an investment property for $250,000.

	Price	Mortgage	Rent	Repayments
Property 1	$250,000	$200,000	$12,500 p.a.	$8,000 p.a.

Assuming a rental yield of 5% and interest rates of 4%.

From this first property, this couple will have upwards of $4,500 surplus income to put towards the next deposit from this example.

Step 3: Work towards your next property

Congratulations, you should have your first of three properties. The next step is to work towards property number two!

It is now time to work out your current cash flow and place a target around your next property goal. The whole point of this first property is to get into the property market and generate a positive cash flow. This is why a deposit of 20% is recommended. Due to the positive cash flow that this property should be yielding, you should be able to accumulate either a larger deposit in the same time or the same deposit in a smaller time.

In addition, this property should also get you tax deductions on the mortgage repayments (which should be interest only to maximise the deductibility) and depreciation (depending on when the property was built or renovated) to reduce what you are paying the tax man.

Where to save?

If your structure on the investment loan against property one is set up correctly, you should have what is called an offset account. This is a transaction account linked to the loan on the investment property. As the name says, any funds that you have in here go towards offsetting interest that would be otherwise payable. A simple example of this is say you have a loan of $400,000, but have $100,000 sitting in your offset account, then the bank would only charge you interest on $300,000 of the funds. Offset accounts work differently to re-draw facilities. The major benefit is you can access the funds at any time, just like a regular savings account.

So why save your funds into this account? The major reason is that it will save you interest payments. Even though these will be tax deductible, it is better to forego a tax deduction and save the interest instead. A better way of explaining this is a deduction is only as good as your marginal tax rate. If you earn $100,000 per annum, then every dollar you spend on interest will only reduce your tax bill by $0.39. Therefore, you spend $1 to get $0.39 back.

	Savings account	Offset account
Nominal amount	$10,000	$10,000
Interest rate	2%	4%
Income Earned/Saved	$200	$400
After tax	$122	$400
Forgone tax deduction	$ -	$156
Net benefit	$122	$244

As you can see this works out to be more effective form a cash flow point of view. Using current rates, an interest-bearing facility will earn you maybe 2% income per year, while a loan will cost you 4% of interest per year. The net benefit for you in this situation would be either earning $122 after tax, or saving $244 of your after-tax funds (after you forego a tax deduction).

Leverage can be your friend as well. Depending on what property prices have done in the time period between purchasing the property and looking at buying your second property, you may be able to unlock 80% of the equity in the property by which it has grown. Have a look at the following example where after 12 months, property one has grown in value allowing access to 80% of the growth to be used as further funds for a deposit.

	Price	Mortgage	LVR	Additional equity	New mortgage
Property 1	$260,000	$200,000	77%	$8,000	$208,000

Assuming a growth in the property of 4%.

The way this works is when you are ready to purchase property two, have property one revalued and if it has increased, refinance your loan to access the additional equity. In this example, you would have another $8,000 to put towards a deposit for property two. This is again where the loan structure plays vital importance. If you had fixed your loan, there would be breaking costs involved in this process which could negate any gains made.

This being said, there is no guarantee that property will increase every year, there may be stagnant years depending on the area, but on average, it should increase by at least inflation. Therefore, the one thing that you can control are your savings and generating a positive cash flow on the property.

The following is a little summary of where you can be at after 12 months using the combination of your savings, surplus income from the property along with the potential of unlocking some further equity.

Savings	$31,000
Investment equity	$ 8,000
Property surplus income	$ 4,500
Total deposit	$43,500

Step 4: Buy property 2.

Now that you have property number one under your belt and build up your next deposit, time to look at property 2.

For this property, it is important to start to diversify your holdings. This can be by buying a different type of property (house, townhouse or apartment), different classification (residential, commercial) and in different geographical areas. It is important to not have all of your property held in one location and in one type, as if this market drops then 100% of your investment will be exposed. This is when property managers are worth their weight in fees, as without them there is little chance to be able to purchase property in different states than where you live and still manage them while working full time.

Again, depending on how much deposit you have acquired will determine what price you can look at for property two. The following is an example looking at our couple from before for a 12-month period of savings, surplus income from their property along with the potential to unlock some extra equity.

Talk to your buyers' agent to get them to look for property based on your criteria of price and the potential to generate a positive cash flow. Using the above deposit amount, you would be able to afford a second property of $217,500. So now your property portfolio will look something like the following:

	Price	Mortgage	Rent	Repayments
Property 1	$260,000	$208,000	$13,000 p.a.	$8,320p.a.

| Property 2 | $217,500 | $174,000 | $10,875 p.a. | $6,960 p.a. |

Assuming a rental yield of 5% and interest rates of 4%.

Depending on your situation, it may take you more or less time to save for the deposit on property two, and that is okay. This is just an example strategy on how to build the property portfolio and if you really have to, you can delay the second property purchase by a few months.

As you can start to see, this is a 'rinse and repeat strategy'. Once property two has been purchased, it is back to the drawing board (so to speak) to start accumulating deposit number three.

Step 5: Building deposit number 3

From two positively geared properties, you should have some additional savings capability. Based on this example, this couple has created an additional $8,595 in surplus income from the properties.

Remember to save your deposit effectively! This means placing these funds into an offset account against one of the investment properties. Remember, while this won't earn you an income, it will save you repayments at a higher rate and tax effectively. Anything that you can save is just as good as something you earn and spend.

Towards the end of year three, your portfolio may have grown, allowing the access of additional equity in two properties this time instead of the one. You can start to see that using leverage, the more property you have the more you can unlock as the value increases.

	Price	Mortgage	LVR	Additional equity	New mortgage
Property 1	$270,400	$208,000	77%	$8,320	$216,320
Property 2	$226,200	$174,000	77%	$6,960	$180,960

Assuming a growth in the property of 4%.

Assuming that both of your properties experience an average long term growth in property of 4% then you can unlock a further $15,280 in equity from these towards your next deposit. As previously mentioned, there is no guarantee that this will occur but hey, it may increase by more.

Savings	$ 31,000
Investment equity	$ 15,280
Property surplus income	$ 8,595
Total deposit	$ 54,875

Step 6: Buy property 3

By this stage, you should be a pro at the steps involved in purchasing a property. Just remember the key to building a portfolio is outsourcing to professionals if you are time poor like so many of us.

Work through your criteria again. Remember to try to diversify further towards either a different area or type of property. Based on the above example, you should have around $54,875 in deposit for the next property. This will allow for the purchase of a property in the vicinity of $274,000 helping to generate a better rental return that property two. Also, remember you still want to look for something that is positively geared, and the best way to do that is find something that is relatively undervalued.

By the end of year 3, your portfolio can look something like the following:

	Price	Mortgage	Rent	Repayments
Property 1	$270,400	$216,320	$13,520 p.a.	$8,653 p.a.
Property 2	$226,200	$180,960	$11,310 p.a.	$7,238 p.a.
Property 3	$274,000	$219,200	$13,700 p.a.	$8,768 p.a.

Assuming a rental yield of 5% and interest rates of 4%.

Step 7: You're earning $2,000 per month

You can now call yourself a mini-mogul! You can see that if you put your mind to it you can achieve your goals.

Your overall position after 3 years:

	Price	Mortgage	Rent	Repayments
Property 1	$270,400	$216,320	$13,520 p.a.	$8,653 p.a.
Property 2	$226,200	$180,960	$11,310 p.a.	$7,238 p.a.
Property 3	$274,000	$219,200	$13,700 p.a.	$8,768 p.a.

Assuming a rental yield of 5% and interest rates of 4%.

Net equity	$ 154,120.00
Surplus income	$ 13,870.80

After another 10 years, the properties may look something like this (assuming you retain the interest only loan).

	Price	Mortgage	Rent	Repayments
Property 1	$400,258	$216,320	$20,013 p.a.	$8,653 p.a.
Property 2	$334,831	$180,960	$16,742 p.a.	$7,238 p.a.
Property 3	$405,587	$219,200	$20,279 p.a.	$8,768 p.a.

Assuming a rental yield of 5% and interest rates of 4%.

You can see that the real power of property, nay any growth investment is the growth potential over the long term. While this strategy is only over a 3-year period (relatively a short time period for a growth strategy) the best thing that you can do is keep these properties for the long run.

Where to from here?

Well this is all up to you! For those of you who are slightly more conservative, start paying down your loans. For those of you who love the risk, why not buy some more property? Or use your surplus income to start diversifying into other assets which can generate more income as well, like shares or bonds.

I would suggest either starting to pay down the debt to help increase your overall net equity along with positive cash flow position due to some of the risks laid out below!

What are the risks involved?

There are risks to this strategy which have to be mentioned but luckily most can be mitigated against.

Interest rates rising – In low interest environments it is quite easy to have a property that is positively geared. It becomes less affordable. Banks stress test at around 7% in interest rates when assessing your servicing ability on a property. If rates do start to rise off the back of the overall economy doing better, then the surplus income your property will generate will decline. Depending on how much rent you can demand, it may even become negatively geared and cost you money. This is why paying down debt is an important strategy in preparation for interest rate movements.

Property price decline –This strategy is using leverage/debt to help piggy back off the growth of a property. This does create a risk if property prices were to decline and you are left with more debt than your properties are worth. This is why we are recommending starting out small in an undervalued area. A good example of what not to do is the story of anyone who bought property in small mining towns with over-inflated property values. They bought property all in the same area for more than it was worth and were exposed to the external risk of the only reason people were living in the area is to get stuff out of the ground. As we saw, when the price of this 'stuff' dropped and nobody could afford to get it out of the ground at past profits, companies moved out of the area and property prices dropped as heavily as the commodity prices.

This movement is referred to as volatility which is often referred to as 'market risks'. This is dependent on the supply and demand relationship we have talked about in a previous episode, so if you haven't, go check it out.

There are ways to mitigate this risk though. Buying property in diverse areas, so different states and even different types of property. Why not buy some commercial property rather than only residential! As always, you make money on the buy so look for something that is undervalued and unlock its true potential.

Job or income loss – Your ability to save is reliant on your income producing ability. If you lose your job or go on maternity leave (assuming unpaid) then the strategy may fall apart. It is important to protect yourself as much as possible. You can purchase Income Protection to make sure that if you suffer an illness or accident income is still coming in. It is harder to protect against job loss. If you work on contracts or have low job stability, this strategy may not be for you.

Inability to get a loan – If you have bad credit history or are having difficulty obtaining a loan from a bank due to incomes, assets or any number of reasons a bank gives then this strategy will be hard to implement. You may be eligible to purchase your first property relatively easily, but as soon as you apply for the loan you are declined by the bank.

Talk to a mortgage broker first to assess what your overall borrowing capability looks like to avoid running into this problem halfway through the strategy!

Conclusion

Time to get started....

We hope you now feel as pumped as we do on building your investment portfolio! Just remember this strategy is just the beginning of your wealth building future!

Stay in touch with us via:

Facebook: http://www.facebook.com/therentvestingpodcast/

Website: http://www.therentvestingpodcast.com.au/

If you liked this book, please post a review at Amazon, and let your friends know about The Rentvesting Podcast.

www.ingramcontent.com/pod-product-compliance
Lightning Source LLC
Chambersburg PA
CBHW032311240526
45464CB00023BA/2982